the
vegetarian
cookbook

DK

Penguin Random House

Senior editor Carrie Love
Senior designer Rachael Parfitt Hunt
Designers Eleanor Bates, Rachael Hare,
Karen Hood, Hannah Moore
Editorial assistant Becky Walsh
Recipe writers Heather Whinney and
Denise Smart
Nutritionist Fiona Hunter
Home economist Denise Smart
Photographer Dave King
Pre-production producers Sophie Chatellier
and Jennifer Murray
Producer John Casey
Jacket designers Sonny Flynn and
Rachael Parfitt Hunt
Jacket co-ordinator Issy Walsh
Managing editor Penny Smith
Managing art editor Mabel Chan
Creative director Helen Senior
Publishing director Sarah Larter

This edition published in 2019 by
Dorling Kindersley Limited
80 Strand, London, WC2R 0RL

A CIP catalogue record for this book is
available from the British Library.

ISBN: 978-0-2414-0702-8
Printed and bound in China

A WORLD OF IDEAS:
SEE ALL THERE IS TO KNOW

www.dk.com

Contents

Brilliant breakfasts

Super snacks

Lovely lunches

Delicious drinks

Moreish main meals

Sweet stuff

Kitchen rules

Cooking is meant to be fun and a little bit messy, but you still need to keep safety and cleanliness in mind. Follow instructions carefully, gather everything together, and read through these rules and tips before you begin.

INGREDIENTS AND EQUIPMENT

• Make sure you have all your ingredients laid out before you start to make a recipe. You'll probably have most ingredients in your kitchen already, but some you will need to buy.

• Always use the type of flour specified in a recipe – strong, plain, or self-raising.

• Use medium-sized free range eggs unless stated otherwise.

• For recipes that require milk, you can use whole milk, semi-skimmed, skimmed, or plant-based. For cheese, use vegan cheese or dairy cheese that isn't made with rennet.

Preheating the oven
Follow the temperature instructions within each recipe.

Special equipment
Keep an eye out for recipes that require special equipment. Buy or borrow items in advance if you don't own them.

WEIGHTS AND MEASUREMENTS

Carefully weigh out the ingredients before you start a recipe. Use measuring spoons, weighing scales, and a measuring jug as necessary. Below are the abbreviations and full names for the measurements used in this book.

Metric	US measures	Spoon measures
g = gram	oz = ounce	tsp = teaspoon
kg = kilogram	lb = pound	tbsp = tablespoon
ml = millilitre	fl oz = fluid ounce	
cm = centimetre	in = inch	

GETTING STARTED

1

Read a recipe all the way through before you start.

2

Wash your hands, put on an apron, and tie back your hair.

3

Make sure you have all the ingredients and equipment on hand before you begin cooking.

KITCHEN SAFETY

Be very careful...

• Around hot ovens, and gas or electric cookers, making sure you know whether the oven or cooker is on, and protecting your hands when touching or lifting anything hot from, or on, or into it. Oven gloves are your friends here!

• Handling hot liquids or hot pans, watching carefully for spillages, and protecting your hands (using oven gloves or a tea towel) when moving or holding hot items. Use a mesh frying pan cover when cooking with hot oil. Tell an adult immediately if you get a burn.

• Handling anything sharp, such as knives or a grater. Take extra care when cutting a large fruit or vegetable that has a thick or hard peel, such as a watermelon, pumpkin, or butternut squash. Cut it into quarters first to make the task safer. Then cut off the peel before chopping the flesh into chunks.

• Using power tools such as blenders, food processors, mixers, and microwaves. Check if they're on, and don't put your hands near the moving parts until you have switched them off at the socket.

• Always wash your hands thoroughly after handling chilli peppers, jalapeños, and chilli flakes and avoid touching your eyes, mouth or other sensitive areas.

IF IN DOUBT ask an ADULT to help, especially when you're unsure about anything.

MAKES/SERVES

This lists the amount of portions a recipe makes or how many people it serves.

PREP/CHILL/REST/ SOAK/RISE/PROVE/ CHURN/FREEZE

This tells you how many minutes and hours a recipe will take to prepare. It includes specific times for extra preparation, such as chilling and rising. Remember that preparation times might be a little longer if it's the first time you're making a recipe.

COOK

This tells you how long it will take to cook a dish.

KITCHEN HYGIENE

Please note that when you're in the kitchen, you need to follow these important rules to keep germs in check.

• Always wash your hands before you start any recipe.

• Wash all fruit and vegetables.

• Use hot, soapy water to clean chopping boards after each use.

• Store raw and cooked food separately.

• Keep your cooking area clean and have a cloth handy to mop up any spillages.

• Always check the use-by date on all ingredients.

• Wash your hands after handling raw eggs.

• **Please note** that the Zingy lime pie and Hollandaise sauce contain egg that isn't fully cooked. Don't serve either to a baby, an elderly person or a pregnant woman.

Equipment

This handy guide features all the special equipment used in this book. Make sure you have the right equipment ready before cooking.

Find it!

Cups

Small bowls

Glasses

Grater

Electric whisk

Ladle

Slotted spoon

Masher

Serrated knife

Sharp knives

Pizza cutter

Basting brush

Peeler

Garlic crusher

Whisks

Kitchen scissors

Ice cream scoop

Mesh frying pan cover

Muffin tin and paper cases

Colander

Sieve

Cutting board

Pie dish

Oven dish

Baking dish

Baking trays, baking sheet

Mixer

Wire rack

Piping bag and
nozzles

Measuring spoons

Plastic container

Measuring cups

Blender, Food
processor

Glass jug

Pizza tray

Flour shaker

Bamboo steamer

Paper straws

Measuring
jug

Cocktail
shaker

Zester

Muddler

Lemon juicer

Glass bowls

Large bowl

Chopsticks

Plastic
spatulas

Wooden
spoon

Wooden
spatulas

Spoons

Table
knife

Fork

Skewers

Cocktail
sticks

Rolling pin

Foil

Milk pan

Heavy-
based
saucepan

Baking parchment

Griddle pan

Frying pans

Cling film

Large saucepan

Wok

Plastic
gloves

Oven
gloves

Healthy eating

The secret to a healthy vegetarian diet is balance. Your body needs more than 40 different nutrients to keep it healthy. This circle shows the proportion of food you need to eat from each food group. No single food provides all the nutrients your body needs, so it's important to eat a variety of different types of food every day.

Fruit and vegetables

These provide vitamins, minerals, phytochemicals (a chemical compound found in plants), and fibre. You need to eat at least five servings a day.

Water

It's not just the food on your plate that's important, you need to drink between 6-8 glasses of fluid a day – water is the healthiest choice.

Proteins

Beans, nuts, and seeds are a vital source of protein, which is essential for the growth and repair of cells in your body.

Potatoes, bread, rice, pasta, and other starchy carbohydrates

To help you get the right balance and all the nutrients you need, nutritionists divide food into different groups. You don't need to eat the exact balance of nutrients at every meal, but you should try to get the balance right, as shown, over one day, as much as possible.

Eat up!

Did you know?

Amino acids are the building blocks that make up protein. The body cannot make some of them, so they need to be provided by the food you eat.

Potatoes, bread, rice, pasta, and other starchy carbohydrates

Bread, cereal, potatoes, rice, pasta, and grains are high in carbohydrates, which gives your body energy. Wholegrain options, like wholemeal bread, are the healthiest choice.

Oils and spreads

Fat is found in oils and spreads. It is essential in your diet, but don't eat too much of it and choose healthy fats, such as avocados and olive oil.

Oils

Dairy

Dairy

Foods such as milk, cheese, and yogurt provide calcium, which helps give us strong bones and teeth. They also contain protein, vitamins A, B2, and B12.

Parsnips
They are a good source of fibre and also provide you with the B vitamin called folate.

Carrots
As an excellent source of vitamin A, carrots help to keep your skin and eyes healthy.

Rocket
Deep green salad leaves, such as rocket, contain more vitamins than lighter leaves.

Celery
Due to its high water content, celery can help keep you hydrated. It's also rich in vitamins A, C, and K.

Vegetables
Try to eat a variety of veggies to get lots of different nutrients. Some of the foods on these pages are actually fruit, but sold as veg.

Mushrooms
Just three handfuls of sliced mushrooms count as one of your five-a-day.

Onions
The fibre in onions encourages friendly bacteria to grow in your gut.

Broccoli
This is an excellent source of vitamins C and K, as well as the B vitamin folate.

Kale
These tasty leaves are rich in vitamins A, C, and K, as well as phytochemicals, which help to keep your eyes healthy.

Spinach
Packed with folate, vitamin C, and potassium, spinach helps to keep your blood, immune system, and eyes healthy.

Cauliflowers
Rich in vitamin K, cauliflowers help to keep your bones healthy.

Beetroot
These are rich in folate, which helps your body make red blood cells and keeps your immune system healthy.

Peppers
Peppers are a fruit. All peppers are super rich in vitamins A and C. Half of a red pepper contains more vitamin C than an orange.

Butternut squash
These are a fruit. They're rich in phytochemicals, called carotenoids, which can help make your skin look healthier.

Peas
Peas are a useful source of iron for vegetarians.

Sweet potatoes
Unlike regular white potatoes, sweet potatoes count towards your five-a-day target.

Cucumbers
Cucumbers are a fruit. Just a 5cm (2incm) piece of cucumber counts as one of your five-a-day.

Pumpkins
Pumpkins are a fruit. They're a great source of betacarotene, which the body can use to make vitamin A.

Watermelons

These are rich in vitamin B6, which you need for a healthy immune system.

Oranges

Super-rich in vitamin C, oranges are also a good source of the B vitamins called B1 and folate.

Figs

Both fresh and dried figs are rich in fibre and make a healthy snack.

Mangoes

These are rich in betacarotene, which helps to keep your skin and eyes healthy.

Fruit

Fruit comes in a rainbow of colours. Each one has a distinct nutritional profile. Try eating a variety of colours every week.

Raisins

Rich in fibre, these are a delicious treat, but limit the amount you eat as they are high in sugar.

Avocados

These are packed with vitamins E and B6, as well as healthy fats and fibre.

Lemons
Packed with vitamin C, lemons help the body to use iron from other foods.

Peaches
You will get around half the recommended daily amount of vitamin C from one medium peach.

Apples
As a good source of fibre, apples help to keep your digestive system healthy.

Limes
If you add lime or lemon juice to flavour your food, you need to add less salt.

Tomatoes
These are actually a fruit, not a vegetable! There are over 5,000 different varieties.

Blueberries
These are packed with phytochemicals - which help to keep your eyes, brain, and heart healthy.

Pineapples
These are a great source of fibre and vitamin C.

Raspberries
Raspberries are rich in manganese and vitamin K, which both play a role in bone health.

Strawberries
These are rich in vitamin C and the B vitamin folate.

Apricots
These contain betacarotene, which your body can convert into vitamin A.

Kiwis
These contain a phytochemical called lutein, which keeps your eyes healthy.

13

Rice
Brown rice contains three times more fibre than white rice.

Pitta breads
These are excellent toasted and eaten with dips. They are a quick and easy source of energy.

Starchy carbohydrates

Try to include these great sources of starchy carbohydrates at every meal – high fibre or wholegrain varieties are best. Carbs give your body energy.

Oats
Oats are a great choice for breakfast, because they release energy slowly over the morning.

Barley
Barley is higher in fibre than white, brown, and wild rice.

Breads
Bread gives your body energy. Whole grain varieties are highest in vitamins, minerals, and fibre.

Pasta
Pasta can be eaten hot, or cold in salads. Wholemeal pasta is best for you as it's higher in fibre.

Noodles

There are many types of noodles. If you don't eat eggs, choose rice noodles instead which are also gluten free.

Quinoa

This healthy seed contains three times more iron than brown rice.

Tortilla wraps

These are filling and make an easy lunch. Choose wholegrain varieties, for extra fibre.

Potatoes

Rich in vitamin C and potassium, potatoes also contain fibre, which is mostly found in the skin.

Wholemeal flour

This contains more fibre and B vitamins than white flour.

Sweet potatoes

Delicious roasted, mashed, or served as wedges, sweet potatoes are a good source of vitamins A and C.

Couscous

This can be eaten hot or cold. Choose wholegrain couscous whenever you can.

Bulgur wheat

This is a good alternative to couscous, because it releases energy more slowly.

15

Halloumi cheese

Unlike other cheese halloumi doesn't melt, when it is heated. It is good served alongside roast vegetables.

Plain yogurt

150g (5½oz) yogurt is a quarter of your daily calcium intake and almost half of your daily iodine intake.

Milk

As well as calcium, milk is a source of protein, iodine, vitamins A, B2, and B12.

Vegetarian hard cheese

Use this instead of Parmesan cheese.

Vegetarian cheese

Some cheeses are made with enzymes from the inside of a cow's stomach, called rennet. For true vegetarian cheese, look for cheese made without rennet or with non-animal rennet.

Feta cheese

This cheese is high in salt, so use it sparingly!

Dairy

Dairy foods are rich in calcium, which makes your bones strong. If you don't eat dairy products, make sure you eat other calcium-rich foods.

Cheddar cheese

This is a good source of vitamins A, B12, and the minerals calcium and phosphorus.

Smoothies

Ready-made smoothies can contain added sugar so it's best to make your own by blending fresh fruit with milk or yogurt.

Plant milk

If you choose a plant-based milk instead of cow's milk, choose one that has calcium and vitamin D added.

Flavourings

Basil
These aromatic leaves add flavour to many Italian dishes and are used to make pesto.

Coriander
This herb is used in lots of Mexican dishes. It tastes great in dips and salads.

Mint
These refreshing leaves are very versatile – add them to a drink or eat with veggies.

Chives
Snip these lightly onion-flavoured stems into yogurt dips, salads, or soups.

Parsley
Stir or sprinkle these leaves into casserole or rice dishes. They add a fresh flavour.

Bay leaf
Cook with these fragrant leaves to bring out some delicious flavours. Then remove before eating.

Turmeric
This strongly scented, bright yellow spice is often used in Indian cooking.

Paprika
This rich spice has a mild chilli flavour that enhances lots of dishes.

Cumin
Add a pinch of this warming, pungent spice to your curry to add extra flavour.

Chilli flakes
At the start of cooking, add a sprinkle of chilli flakes to give a fiery flavour to your dish.

Salt
A pinch of salt will enhance the flavour of your food. Ensure you use it sparingly.

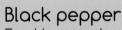

Black pepper
Freshly ground black pepper adds a depth of flavour to any savoury dish.

Vinegar
Mix a splash with olive oil to make a salad dressing with a kick.

Lemon
A squeeze of tangy lemon juice over food provides vitamin C.

Lime
This sharp, zingy citrus flavour goes well with spicy dishes.

Clove
A very aromatic spice, cloves add a warming, spicy flavour to food.

Cinnamon
Cinnamon sticks can be used in both savoury and sweet dishes.

Garlic
Cook with onions to add a punchy flavour to all savoury dishes.

Ginger
A zesty spice used in Asian cooking, it's super tasty in a stir-fry.

Pumpkin seeds
As well as protein, these are a good source of zinc.

Almonds
These are rich in calcium, which is very important if you don't eat dairy foods.

Cheese
All types of cheese are rich in protein, but they also provide B vitamins and calcium.

Proteins
Lots of foods provide protein. Eating a variety of foods from this group will help you get your essential amino acids.

Pistachio nuts
As well as protein, all nuts provide healthy fats.

Peanut butter
As well as protein, peanut butter is a good source of healthy fats.

Beans
All beans are packed with protein. Just three heaped tablespoons count as one of your five-a-day.

Cashew nuts
Cashews are rich in zinc and vitamins E and K. When blended, they make a creamy base for dips and dressings.

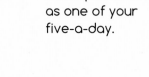

Chickpeas

Canned chickpeas are quick and easy to use, and just as nutritious as dried ones, which require more time to prepare. Just make sure you rinse them first!

Milk

This provides protein in your diet, but is also a good source of calcium which is important for strong and healthy bones.

Pine nuts

These contain protein and vitamin E. They also contain vitamin K, which helps keep blood healthy.

Lentils

As well as being high in protein, lentils are rich in fibre and B vitamins.

Eggs

On top of protein, eggs contain other nutrients, including vitamins B12 and D, as well as iodine.

Fibre

Fruit and Veg

Fresh, frozen, and dried fruit all provide good amounts of fibre. All veggies provide fibre.

Oats

These contain a type of fibre which helps to keep your heart and your digestive system healthy.

Wholegrains

As well as fibre, wholegrain foods contains more vitamins and minerals than 'white' carbs.

Beans

All beans, including baked beans, and hummus, which is made from chickpeas, are a good source of fibre.

Nuts and seeds

All nut and seed products, like nut butters, are also rich in fibre.

Potatoes

Most of the fibre in potatoes is found in the skin, so try eating potatoes with their skin on.

Brilliant
breakfasts

Dig in!

Whether you're a morning person or not, it's important to eat a nutritious breakfast to set you up for the day. Wake up to a tasty Bircher muesli, make a simple avocado mash, flip pancakes with a veggie twist, or make absolutely perfect eggs!

Avocado mash on sourdough toast

Creamy avocado mash is a filling and tasty start for any morning. It's really easy and quick to make. Leave out the chilli flakes if you're not into spicy food.

chilli flakes

In a large bowl, add the avocado, lemon juice, and chia seeds. Season well with the salt and pepper. Gently mash the ingredients with the back of a fork. Spread over the warm toast. Sprinkle over the coriander leaves and chilli flakes, if using.

salt and pepper

22

coriander

sourdough bread

Ingredients

2 avocados, halved
and pitted

juice of 1 lemon

2 tsp chia seeds

sea salt and freshly ground
black pepper

4 chunky slices of sourdough
bread, toasted

handful of coriander leaves

sprinkle of chilli flakes
(optional)

avocado

chia seeds

lemon

Scrambled
eggs

Once you've mastered this delicious recipe you can start to add other flavours and ingredients to make your perfect eggs.

Ingredients

50g (1¾oz) butter

2 eggs

4 tbsp milk

sea salt and freshly ground black pepper

4 slices of multigrain bread, toasted and buttered, to serve

2 tsp chives, chopped, to serve (optional)

SERVES 2
PREP 5 MINS
COOK 5 MINS

1

Heat the butter in a non-stick frying pan, until just foaming. In a bowl, lightly whisk the eggs and milk together. Season well.

Try this!
Once the eggs are cooked, stir through a handful of chopped fresh tomatoes or a few cooked mushrooms and a sprinkling of grated cheese.

2

Pour the mixture into the pan and leave it for a few seconds, then, using a wooden spatula, begin to fold it over and stir gently. Leave it to sit again, then fold it over.

3

Remove the pan from the heat just before the eggs are cooked – they should still be wet and wobbly. The eggs will continue to cook in the pan for a minute. Stir again and serve on the toast. Sprinkle with chives, if using.

stir it!

Mango yogurt with toast dippers

This is a simple and healthy way to start the day – the juicy mango is delicious with yogurt. You can sweeten with a drizzle of honey and toasted coconut, if you like.

yogurt

Spoon a little yogurt into two bowls, then add the chopped mango. Sprinkle with toasted coconut and drizzle with honey, if using. Slice the brioche into fingers and serve with the yogurt.

coconut

brioche

Ingredients

200g (7oz) Greek natural yogurt

1 mango, halved, pitted, and chopped

2 slices of brioche, lightly toasted

2 small pieces of fresh coconut, sliced and toasted (optional)

drizzle of runny honey (optional)

honey

mango

27

Crunchy, sweet pancakes

These delicious pancakes have all the flavours of a carrot cake! They are perfect for breakfast or as a dessert, served with some ice cream.

MAKES 12
PREP 12 MINS
COOK 15 MINS

28

1

Add the flour, baking powder, salt, sugar, and cinnamon to a large bowl and mix together.

2

In another bowl, whisk the eggs and milk together, then pour it into the flour mixture and beat to form a batter.

3

Add the grated carrot and sultanas to the mixture. Gently fold in until evenly distributed.

4

Heat a drizzle of oil in a non-stick frying pan. When hot, add a dollop of batter to the pan. You should be able to cook three at a time.

5

Cook for 2-3 minutes, then flip using a spatula and cook the other side for a further 2-3 minutes. Move to a plate and cook the remaining pancakes. Serve with a drizzle of maple syrup.

Ingredients

175g (6oz) plain flour

2 tsp baking powder

pinch of sea salt

25g (scant 1oz) caster sugar

1 tsp ground cinnamon

3 eggs

150ml (5fl oz) full-fat milk

2 carrots, grated and squeezed to remove water

handful of sultanas

vegetable oil, for frying

drizzle of maple syrup, to serve

ice cream, to serve (optional)

golden brown

Bircher
muesli

This sweet breakfast treat is made from oats soaked in apple juice overnight and a delicious mix of fruit and nuts. It's a tasty way to start the day!

milk

raspberries

In a large bowl, add the oats, dried fruits, and apple juice. Leave to soak overnight. In another bowl, mix the grated apple and milk, then stir into the soaked oats. Sprinkle over the nuts and a spoonful of yogurt, then scatter over raspberries and drizzle over some honey to serve.

apricots

figs

30

yogurt

honey

Ingredients

50g (1¾oz) oats

2 tbsp dried apricots, chopped

2 tbsp dried figs, chopped

8–10 tbsp apple juice

1 apple, grated

splash of milk

handful of almonds, roughly chopped

1 heaped tbsp Greek yogurt, to serve

handful of raspberries, to serve

runny honey, to serve

oats

almonds

apple juice

grated apple

Poached eggs with greens and hollandaise sauce

Served with the lemony, buttery hollandaise sauce, poached eggs are a great dish for a weekend breakfast.

SERVES 2
PREP 15 MINS
COOK 20 MINS

1 For the hollandaise sauce, melt the butter in a small pan and put aside.

2

In a heatproof bowl, add the egg yolk, vinegar, salt, and a sprinkle of ice-cold water. Put the bowl over a pan of simmering water. Whisk continuously until the mixture starts to thicken. Take off the heat, whisk in the butter, and add the lemon juice. Set aside.

Ingredients

For the hollandaise sauce

60g (2oz) butter

1 egg yolk

¼ tsp white balsamic vinegar

pinch of sea salt

squeeze of lemon juice

For the poached eggs

200g (7oz) spring green cabbage, or spinach leaves

2 eggs

4 slices of bread muffin, toasted

pinch of paprika, to serve

* Please note: the hollandaise sauce contains egg that isn't fully cooked.

3

Steam the cabbage or spinach in a metal colander over a pan of simmering water. Season with salt. Put a lid on and cook for 2 minutes, or until tender. Set aside and keep warm.

4

Crack an egg into a cup. Boil a pan of water and swirl it with a spoon to make a gentle whirlpool. Slowly pour the egg into the center of the whirlpool. Cook for 3–4 minutes, until the white is cooked. Use a slotted spoon to remove the eggs.

5 Put the greens on the muffin slices and top with an egg. Drizzle with the sauce. Sprinkle with paprika and serve.

Super snacks

When you're feeling peckish, reach for tasty cheesy muffins and fresh salad bowls. Then, dip into delicious flatbreads, sweet potato fries, homemade nachos, sliced veg, plantain chips, and Chinese rolls!

Flatbreads and dips

Make one or all of these yummy dips to serve with the flatbreads. Which one is your favourite?

MAKES 6
PREP 25 MINS
COOK 25 MINS

Ingredients

- 175g (6oz) self-raising flour, plus extra for dusting
- 1 tsp baking powder
- 175g (6oz) natural yogurt

1

In a large bowl, add the flour, baking powder, and yogurt.

2

Using your hands, bring everything together to form a dough.

3

Tip the dough out onto a lightly floured surface and knead for a few minutes.

4

Put the dough in a bowl and leave for 15 minutes. Carefully cut it in half, then cut each half into three, and roll into balls.

On a lightly floured surface, roll each ball into a 10cm (4in) round.

5

One at a time, carefully put the rounds in a hot griddle pan and cook for 2 minutes each side until pale golden. Remove and serve warm with the dips.

Whizz!

Cashew dip

Soak 125g (4½oz) cashews in water for 2 hours. Whizz 100ml (3½fl oz) extra virgin olive oil, 2 garlic cloves, 1 tbsp balsamic vinegar, seasoning, and the cashews in a food processor. Add a little water if needed. Top with snipped chives to serve.

— mix well

Baba ganoush

Prick 2 aubergines all over with a fork, then grill for 15 minutes, until tender. When cool, remove the skin and put the flesh in a bowl with 2 grated garlic cloves, 1-2 tbsp tahini, juice of ½ lemon, 2 tbsp extra virgin olive oil, and seasoning. Mix well.

Blitz!

Red pepper hummus

Add a drained 350g (12oz) jar of roasted red peppers, 2 x 400g (14oz) cans of drained chickpeas, 2-3 tbsp extra virgin olive oil, pinch of ground cumin, 2 garlic cloves, and seasoning to a food processor and blitz. Add a little water if too thick.

Plantain chips **and dips**

This is such an easy snack to make ahead and then enjoy with your friends.

SERVES 4
PREP 15 MINS
COOK 20 MINS

Ingredients

2 green plantains, or unripe green bananas

2 tsp extra virgin olive oil

salt and freshly ground black pepper

1

Preheat the oven to 200°C (400°F/Gas 6). Peel the plantains or bananas and thinly slice them carefully.

2

Coat it!

Line a baking tray with baking parchment. In a bowl, coat the plantain in the oil and season well. Place on the tray.

3

Bake for 20 minutes, or until golden. The chips should just be beginning to crisp. Transfer to a bowl and serve with the dips.

Mix it!

lemon juice

paprika

Garlic and lemon yogurt dip

In a bowl, mix together 200g (7oz) Greek yogurt, juice of 1 lemon, pinch of sea salt, pinch of paprika, and 3 garlic cloves, grated. Spoon into a serving dish. Top with a few gratings of lemon zest.

red chillies

lime juice

Lime and chilli mayonnaise dip

In a bowl, mix together juice of 1 lime, 1 tsp paprika, 6 tbsp mayonnaise, and 1 chilli, finely chopped. Season with black pepper and salt. Spoon into a serving dish. Dust with another 1 tsp paprika.

Warm and fruity
bulgur wheat salad

A colourful, hot grain salad with Moroccan spices – a super easy dish to make ahead.

SERVES 4
PREP 15 MINS
COOK 10 MINS

40

1 Put the bulgur wheat and a pinch of salt in a pan. Pour over boiling water up to about 5cm (2in) above the bulgur. Simmer gently with the lid on for 5-6 minutes. Turn the heat off and leave to steam a little with the lid on. Fluff up, using a fork. Move to a large bowl.

Stir!

2 Heat the oil in a frying pan, add the red onion, spices, and season well. Cook for 2-3 minutes then stir in the garlic and peppers. Cook for a few minutes more until the peppers are softened. Tip into the bulgur wheat and stir.

Ingredients

300g (10oz) bulgur wheat

sea salt and freshly ground black pepper

1 tbsp olive oil

1 red onion, finely chopped

pinch of ground cinnamon

pinch of ground cumin

2 garlic cloves, finely chopped

1 red pepper and 1 yellow pepper, halved, deseeded, and finely chopped

400g (14oz) can chickpeas, drained, rinsed, and cooked carefully in boiling water for 4 minutes

handful of raisins

handful of shelled, raw pistachio nuts, roughly chopped

bunch of coriander, chopped

bunch of mint, chopped

2 oranges, chopped into bite-sized pieces

For the dressing

3 tbsp extra virgin olive oil

1 tbsp white balsamic vinegar

sea salt and freshly ground black pepper

3 Add the chickpeas, raisins, pistachio nuts, and herbs and give it a thorough stir. Season again, if needed.

4 Stir through the dressing and lightly stir through the orange pieces. Serve warm.

Mix it!

For the dressing, add the oil and vinegar to a small bowl or jug, season with sea salt and freshly ground black pepper, and whisk together.

41

Chinese rolls

MAKES 24
PREP 30 MINS
CHILL 15 MINS

These are really simple to make as you do not need to cook these fresh spring rolls. You can be as adventurous as you like with the filling.

1

Fill a large bowl with cold water and add the rice paper wrappers one at a time.

2

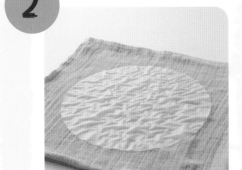

Pat with your hands until they start to feel just pliable; don't soak too long or they will tear. Sit the paper wrappers on a damp, clean tea towel.

3

Top each wrapper with a few leaves first. Then, top with some of the beansprouts, peppers, carrots, spring onions, and cucumber. Sprinkle over a few herbs.

Ingredients

24 rice paper wrappers, about 22cm (8½in)

large handful of mixed leaves

200g (7oz) beansprouts

2 red peppers, deseeded and sliced into fine strips

2 carrots, peeled and sliced into fine strips

bunch of spring onions, trimmed, halved, and finely sliced lengthways

1 cucumber, halved lengthways, seeds removed, and sliced into fine strips

handful of fresh basil leaves

handful of fresh mint leaves

For the dipping sauce

4 tbsp dark soy sauce

2 garlic cloves, finely chopped

1 small red chilli, finely chopped

1 tbsp finely chopped fresh ginger

2 tsp golden caster sugar

juice of 1 lime

4

Bring the bottom of the wrapper up over the filling and roll tightly.

5

Fold the edges in and continue rolling until it is good and tight. Repeat with all the remaining wrappers.

Put all the ingredients for the dipping sauce into a bowl, mix well, and serve with the rolls. When ready to serve, carefully slice each roll across in half and arrange on a large plate with the dipping sauce.

Crudités
and dips

Crudités are raw veggies, and this is an easy, fun way to eat up your five-a-day. Be as adventurous as you want with your choice of veg – if it's good eaten raw, chop it and add it to the selection.

Spoon the dips into individual serving bowls, put them on a large platter or board and serve with the crudités.

pepper

In a bowl, mix 200ml (7fl oz) soured cream, a splash of milk, 1 tsp balsamic vinegar, a small handful of chopped chives, parsley, and dill, and season with sea salt and freshly ground black pepper.

celery

Soured cream and herb dip

Yogurt and feta dip

In a bowl, beat together 200g (7oz) Greek yogurt with 200g (7oz) feta cheese, mix in the juice of ½ lemon, a sprinkle of chilli flakes, and season with freshly ground black pepper.

Ingredients

3 carrots, peeled and cut into baton shapes

3 peppers, a mix of red, yellow and orange, deseeded and cut into strips

bunch of celery, trimmed and cut into baton shapes

handful of sugarsnap peas

1 cucumber, deseeded and cut into baton shapes

cucumber

carrot

Add a 300g (10oz) pack ready cooked beetroot to a food processor and whizz. Add 4 tbsp crème fraîche or plain yogurt, a pinch of sumac, a small handful of mint leaves and season well with sea salt and freshly ground black pepper. Whizz again until smooth.

sugarsnap peas

Beetroot and mint dip

Homemade
nachos

This sharing platter of homemade nachos, piled high with beans, salsa, and melted cheese, is perfect for a get-together.

Did you know?

Each portion of this dish will provide two portions of vegetables and almost one-third of the total amount of fibre you need each day!

1

Preheat the oven to 200°C (400°F/Gas 6). Lightly brush a large baking tray with the oil. Add the tortilla triangles and sprinkle with paprika. Put in the oven and bake for about 4–5 minutes or until just golden.

2

Mix the avocado in a bowl with the lemon juice.

3

cheese

avocado   refried beans

Spoon the warmed refried beans, avocado, and jalapeños, if using, over the warmed tortilla triangles, and top with the grated cheese. Put back in the oven and bake for a few minutes until the cheese has melted.

4

Top with the salsa, a drizzle of soured cream, and scatter over coriander leaves, if using. Serve with lime wedges.

Ingredients

½ tbsp olive oil, plus extra for brushing

12 wholemeal tortillas, sliced into triangles

pinch of paprika

2 avocados, pitted and roughly chopped

juice of ½ lemon

400g (14oz) can refried beans, gently heated

1 jalapeño, sliced (depending on how hot you like it)

150g (5½oz) cheese, grated

200g (7oz) soured cream, to serve

a few coriander leaves to garnish (optional)

lime wedges, to serve

For the tomato salsa

8 tomatoes, finely diced

1 small onion, diced

2 cloves garlic, finely chopped

1 red chilli, halved, deseeded, and finely chopped

large handful of coriander leaves, chopped

juice of ½ lime

2–3 tsp balsamic vinegar

sea salt and freshly ground black pepper

coriander

tomato

garlic

onion

red chilli

Mix together the ingredients for the salsa in a bowl.

Cheese and herb
muffins

MAKES 10
PREP 15 MINS
COOK 20 MINS

If you are new to baking, these muffins make a good choice as they're super easy to make and wonderfully tasty.

1

Preheat the oven to 200°C (400°F/Gas 6). Line 10 holes in the muffin tin with the paper cases. In a large bowl, put the flour, baking powder, and most of the cheese and mix.

2

Put the spinach in another bowl, cover with cling film, and microwave for 3 minutes. Once cool, chop finely. Put in a bowl with the butter, milk, eggs, chives, and seasoning and mix well.

3

Tip the spinach mixture into the flour and cheese mixture and beat it together with a wooden spoon. Don't worry about any lumps, these will disappear while the muffins bake.

Ingredients

150g (5½oz) self-raising flour

1 tsp baking powder

150g (5½oz) Cheddar cheese, grated

100g (3½oz) baby spinach leaves

25g (scant 1oz) butter, melted

100ml (3½fl oz) milk

2 eggs

handful of chives, finely chopped

sea salt and freshly ground black pepper

Special equipment

12-hole muffin tin

10 paper muffin cases

4 Bake!

Spoon the mixture into the paper cases, sprinkle over the remaining cheese, and bake for 18–20 minutes until the muffins are risen and baked through. They are delicious when eaten warm!

49

Watermelon and feta summer salad

Whip up this sweet and salty dish on a hot, summery day. Serve it as a snack or a light lunch.

feta cheese

pine nuts

Toss it!

In a large salad bowl, gently toss the watermelon, red onion, feta, black-eyed beans, basil, and two-thirds of the pine nuts. In another bowl, mix together the oil and lemon juice for the dressing. Season with black pepper. Drizzle over the salad and serve sprinkled with the rest of the pine nuts.

50

basil leaves

red onion

Ingredients

½ small watermelon, peeled carefully, cut into quarters, deseeded, and chopped

½ small red onion, thinly sliced

125g (4½oz) feta cheese, crumbled

420g (15½oz) can black-eyed beans in water, rinsed and drained

large handful of basil leaves, roughly torn

30g (1oz) pine nuts

For the dressing

2 tsp olive oil

juice of ½ lemon

freshly ground black pepper

black-eyed beans

watermelon

Parsnip and
sweet potato fries

Switch regular potato fries for a sweeter and more nutritious version. They are great served on their own or with a main meal.

Ingredients

400g (14oz) parsnips, peeled

400g (14oz) sweet potatoes, peeled

2 tbsp olive oil

2 garlic cloves, crushed

pinch of paprika

pinch of sea salt and freshly ground black pepper

mayonnaise, to serve

tomato sauce, serve

Chop it!

Make the fries as thick or thin as you like.

SERVES 4
PREP 15 MINS
COOK 30 MINS

1 Preheat the oven to 200°C (400°F/Gas 6). Carefully chop the parsnips and sweet potatoes into fry shapes.

2

Tip the fries into a large bowl and add the oil, garlic, paprika, and seasoning. Toss well together.

3

Put the fries on a baking tray and cook in the oven for 20–30 minutes until golden. Keep a watcheful eye as they can burn quickly. Serve warm with mayonnaise and tomato sauce.

Lovely
lunches

Dip in!

Feast on these tasty dishes from around the world. From Mexican veggie wraps and quesadillas, to Italian frittata, risotto, and pesto pasta – they're all filling and full of flavour. They will load you with energy to keep going all afternoon.

Vegetable wraps

Everyone loves Mexican-style wraps, and this veggie version is packed with loads of flavour!

Ingredients

1 red onion, roughly chopped

1 red pepper and 1 orange pepper, halved, deseeded and roughly chopped

pinch of ground cumin

pinch of paprika

sea salt and freshly ground black pepper

2 tbsp olive oil

200g (7oz) halloumi, sliced

large handful of mixed leaves

4 large flour tortillas, warmed

2 tomatoes, chopped

1 tbsp chipotle sauce

4 tbsp natural yogurt

2 limes, cut into wedges

handful of coriander leaves

For the guacamole

3 avocados, pitted and roughly chopped

handful of fresh coriander leaves

juice of ½ lime

1 tomato, finely chopped

SERVES 4
PREP 15 MINS
COOK 20 MINS

1

Preheat the oven to 200°C (400°F/Gas 6). Put the red onion and peppers in a roasting tin. Sprinkle with the cumin and paprika, season well, drizzle over half the olive oil, and toss together. Roast in the oven for 20 minutes.

2

Meanwhile, toss the halloumi slices with the remaining oil. Heat a griddle pan to hot and carefully add the slices a few at a time. Cook until char lines appear on the underside, then flip and cook the other side for a few seconds.

3

To assemble the wraps, put the leaves down the middle of each tortilla, then top with the roasted onions and peppers, tomatoes, and halloumi. Spoon on some chipotle sauce and guacamole. Add a spoonful of yogurt, squeeze over a little lime juice, and scatter with some coriander. Do not overload or the wraps will be tricky to fold!

4

To fold, pull the top and bottom of the wrap over the filling.

Fold one half of the wrap over the filling, then pull the other half tightly over the top.

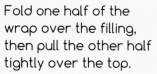

Turn the wrap over so that the folds are face down. Serve immediately.

To make the guacamole, put the avocado, lime juice, coriander leaves, tomato, and some seasoning in a bowl. Mash and stir using a fork until you get a chunky mixture. Cover and keep in the fridge until ready to serve.

Pearl barley
risotto

SERVES 4
PREP 15 MINS
COOK 50 MINS

Risotto is usually made with risotto rice, but pearl barley makes this dish wonderfully chewy and nut-flavoured.

Ask an adult to help you prepare the butternut squash. Be very careful when using a sharp knife. Carefully cut the vegetable into quarters before peeling/cutting the skin off. Then, deseed and chop the flesh into chunks.

Ingredients

1 butternut squash, carefully peeled, deseeded, and cubed

2 tbsp olive oil

salt and freshly ground black pepper

1 onion, finely chopped

2 garlic cloves, finely chopped

300g (10oz) pearl barley

1 vegetable stock cube, dissolved in 1 litre (1¾ pints) boiling water

handful of spinach leaves

handful of basil leaves, roughly chopped

handful of pine nuts, toasted, or use unsalted, shelled pistachio nuts, toasted

2 tbsp hard cheese, grated, to serve

1 Preheat the oven to 200°C (400°F/Gas 6). Put the squash in a roasting tin, drizzle over half the oil, season well, and toss to coat. Roast in the oven for 20–30 minutes until tender.

2 In a large saucepan, heat the remaining oil. Add the onion, season, and cook for 2 minutes until soft. Stir in the garlic and cook for 1 minute, then tip in the pearl barley and stir well.

3 Carefully add half of the vegetable stock, stir, and simmer for 5 minutes. Mix in the remaining stock, cover with a lid, and simmer for 30 minutes until the pearl barley is tender.

4 Stir in the spinach until it wilts, then mix in the roasted squash, basil, and pine nuts. Serve with the grated cheese sprinkled on top.

Mix it!

Quesadillas

Queso is Spanish for cheese, so that's one ingredient you'll definitely find in this twist on a Mexican quesadilla. This one is loaded with roasted sweet potato.

Did you know?

Beans are a great source of protein if you don't eat meat. Protein helps keep your body healthy and strong.

1

Preheat the oven to 200°C (400°F/Gas 6). Put the sweet potato in a roasting tin, drizzle over a teaspoon of the olive oil, season well, and toss to coat. Roast in the oven for 20 minutes or until tender.

2

Carefully heat the remaining oil in a frying pan over a medium heat. Add the spring onion and green chilli, season well, and cook for 2 minutes. Add the black beans and the roasted sweet potato. Stir and heat through.

3

Heat another large frying pan on a medium heat and carefully add a tortilla. Spread a quarter of the bean mixture on top, then top with cheese and jalapeños (if using).

4

Top with another tortilla, press together, and cook for 3 minutes.

5 Carefully flip the quesadilla and cook the other side until golden. Remove from the pan with a spatula and slice into four triangles. Cook the remaining quesadillas. Serve with a dollop of slaw.

Ingredients

2 sweet potatoes, peeled and cubed

1 tbsp olive oil

salt and freshly ground black pepper

4 spring onions, trimmed and finely chopped

1 green chilli, deseeded and finely chopped

400g (14oz) can black beans, rinsed and drained

8 flour or corn tortillas, warmed

large handful of Cheddar cheese, grated

pickled jalapeño chillies, sliced (optional)

For the slaw

¼ white cabbage, finely chopped

1 carrot, grated

1 apple, grated

2 tbsp extra virgin olive oil

3 tbsp white balsamic vinegar

1 tbsp maple syrup

sprinkle of chilli flakes (optional)

Stir it!

To make the slaw, put the cabbage, carrot, and apple into a large bowl. In a small bowl, mix the oil, vinegar, maple syrup, and chilli flakes (if using). Season, then stir it into the vegetables and apple mix.

Veggie gyoza

MAKES 18
PREP 20 MINS
REST 20 MINS
COOK 30 MINS

Gyoza is the Japanese name for stuffed, half moon-shaped dumplings. These delicious steamed gyoza are super light and fluffy.

Ingredients

300g (10oz) plain flour, plus extra for dusting

200g (7oz) Chinese cabbage

150g (5½oz) mushrooms

2 spring onions

1 tbsp fresh ginger, grated

1 tbsp dark soy sauce

1 tbsp lime juice

½ egg, lightly beaten

sea salt and freshly ground black pepper

For the dipping sauce

2 tbsp dark soy sauce

2 tbsp lime juice

1 tsp caster sugar

1 tsp fresh ginger, grated

Special equipment

steamer – a bamboo one is best for these, but not essential

1

To make the dough, sift the flour into a large bowl. Slowly pour in 180ml (6fl oz) warm water, mixing as you go, until the mixture forms a dough. You may not need all the water.

2

On a lightly floured surface, knead the dough for about 5 minutes, until smooth. Cover with a damp, clean cloth and leave for 20 minutes.

3

To make the filling, whizz the cabbage, mushrooms, and spring onions in a food processor. Tip into a bowl and mix in the ginger, soy sauce, lime juice, and egg. Season well.

4

Carefully cut the dough into three pieces. On a lightly floured surface, roll each piece into a sausage shape.

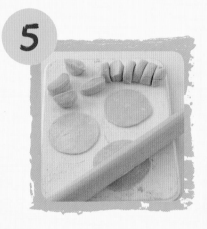

5

Carefully cut each sausage shape into 6 x 2cm (¾in) discs. Roll out each disc of dough into a circle about 10cm (4in) wide.

6

Add a heaped teaspoon of filling to each circle. Dab a little water around the edge. Bring the edges together to make a semicircle. Press together to seal. Repeat with the remaining dough and filling.

7 Line the steamer with parchment paper and sit the dumplings in it. Place the steamer on a wok or large saucepan of boiling water. The water shouldn't touch the food. Put the lid on and steam for about 8–10 minutes. Repeat in batches if you have a small steamer.

In a bowl, whisk together the ingredients for the dipping sauce and serve with the gyoza.

Pumpkin
soup

Perfect for lunch, this rich soup
is even better served with warm
toasted sourdough bread.

1

Carefully heat the oil in a large pan over a medium heat. Add the onion, celery, and bay leaf. Season and cook for 2 minutes. Add the chopped garlic and ginger, then cook for another minute.

2

Stir in the pumpkin or squash and cook for 5 minutes until it begins to soften, stirring occasionally to prevent burning.

3

Carefully pour in the stock, bring to the boil, then reduce to a simmer and cook for 15 minutes, or until tender.

Ingredients

1 tbsp olive oil

1 onion, finely chopped

2 celery sticks, finely chopped

1 bay leaf

pinch of sea salt and freshly ground black pepper

2 garlic cloves, finely chopped

1 tbsp fresh ginger, grated

1kg (2¼lb) pumpkin (or use butternut squash), skin carefully peeled, flesh chopped into chunks, seeds reserved and toasted

1 vegetable stock cube, dissolved in 750ml (1¼ pints) boiling water

4 slices of sourdough bread, toasted, to serve

Ask an adult to help you prepare the pumpkin or butternut squash. Be very careful when using a sharp knife. Carefully cut the vegetable into quarters before peeling/cutting the skin off. Then, deseed and chop the flesh into chunks.

Blitz!

4

Remove the bay leaf. Carefully ladle the mixture into a blender and whizz until smooth. If it's too thick, add a little hot water. Serve in bowls, scatter over the toasted pumpkin seeds, and serve with the sourdough bread.

Vegetable frittata

SERVES 4
PREP 20 MINS
COOK 36 MINS

A frittata is an Italian omelette and this one is loaded with tasty veggies – you can fill it with your favourite veg if you like.

Ingredients

1–2 tbsp olive oil

1 red onion, roughly chopped

sea salt and freshly ground black pepper

½ butternut squash, carefully peeled, deseeded, and cut into small cubes

150g (5½oz) mushrooms, sliced

large handful of kale leaves

large handful of spinach leaves

6 eggs

handful of grated hard cheese

1

Carefully heat the olive oil in a large non-stick frying pan over a medium heat, then add the onion and season well. Cook for 3–4 minutes until softened.

2

Stir in the butternut squash and cook for 8–10 minutes, or until softened. Add more oil if it starts to dry out. Be careful around hot oil.

3

Push the squash to one side of the pan and add the mushrooms. Cook for a further 3 minutes.

4

Add the kale leaves and stir well. Cover with a lid and cook for 5 minutes, then add the spinach to the pan and cook for a further 2 minutes, until wilted.

5

Preheat the grill to medium heat. Mix together the eggs and cheese in a bowl. Season well. Pour the egg mixture evenly over the veg and cook on a low heat for 5–6 minutes. The edges will start to cook first.

6 Carefully put the pan under the grill for 5–6 minutes until the frittata is set and golden. Remove from the heat, leave for 5 minutes, then use a knife to loosen it around the edges and turn it out onto a plate. Slice to serve.

Ask an adult to help you prepare the butternut squash. Be very careful when using a sharp knife. Carefully cut the vegetable into quarters before peeling/cutting the skin off. Then, deseed and chop the flesh into chunks.

Pasta and homemade
pesto

SERVES 4
PREP 20 MINS
COOK 15 MINS

Nothing beats homemade pesto and its fabulous fresh taste. It's so simple to make and absolutely delicious.

Ingredients

large handful of basil leaves

2 tbsp pine nuts, lightly toasted

2 garlic cloves

pinch of sea salt and freshly ground black pepper

100g (3½oz) hard mature cheese, grated

200ml (7fl oz) extra virgin olive oil

400g (14oz) pasta shapes of your choice

1 Put the basil, pine nuts, garlic, and seasoning in a food processor and whizz to form a paste.

Whizz it!

2 Add the cheese to the paste and whizz again.

3 Slowly drizzle in the oil and whizz until it forms a sauce consistency. Add more oil if it is too thick.

4 Carefully boil a large pan of water, then add the pasta and cook for 12 minutes, or follow the pack instructions.

5 Drain the pasta carefully, put it back in the pan, and toss it with the pesto. Serve immediately.

Lentil dhal and paratha bread

This Indian dish is packed with flavour and not too spicy. The paratha is perfect for dipping in the dhal.

Ingredients

For the paratha bread

125g (4½oz) wholemeal flour

125g (4½oz) plain flour

pinch of sea salt

4 tbsp vegetable oil

70g (2¼oz) rice flour, for dusting

For the dhal

200g (7oz) split red lentils, rinsed and drained

sea salt and freshly ground black pepper

1 tbsp olive oil

1 onion, finely chopped

2 garlic cloves, finely chopped

1 tbsp grated fresh ginger

1 red chilli, finely chopped

2 tsp turmeric

400g (14oz) can chopped tomatoes

handful of coriander leaves, roughly chopped

lemon wedges, to serve

SERVES 4
PREP 10 MINS
REST 15 MINS
COOK 50 MINS

1

To make the paratha, put the flours and salt in a large bowl, make a well in the centre, and add 2 tablespoons of the oil. Mix it with your fingers until combined.

2 Roll!

Pour in 160ml (5½fl oz) warm water. Knead to form a dough. Add more water if dry. Roll into a ball, coat in 1 teaspoon of oil. Rest in a bowl, covered with cling film, for 15 minutes.

3 Knead!

Knead the dough for 1 minute, then carefully cut it in half and roll each half into a thick log. Pull 4 pieces from each log and roll each one into a ball, then flatten into a disk.

4

On a surface dusted with a little rice flour, roll out each disk into a 10cm (4in) round. Spread a little oil on each round, then fold into quarters. Press and re-roll into rounds.

5

Heat a cast-iron frying pan over a medium heat. Carefully cook the rounds, one at a time, for 1 minute, until bubbles form. Flip and cook the other side. Set aside in a warm place.

6

To make the dhal, add the lentils to a large pan, pour in 750ml (1¼ pints) water, season well, and simmer for 20 minutes until the lentils are soft.

7

Carefully heat the oil in a large frying pan over a medium heat. Add the onion and season well. Cook for 2-3 minutes until soft. Stir in the garlic, ginger, chilli, and turmeric. Cook for 2 minutes.

8

Tip in the tomatoes and cook on a low heat for 10 minutes, then stir it into the cooked red lentils. Add coriander leaves. Serve with the paratha bread.

71

Easy
veggie rolls

MAKES 12
PREP 15 MINS
COOK 10 MINS

These crunchy, sweet rolls are a quirky twist on sushi. The vinegar gives the rice its tangy flavour.

Dip your rolls in soy sauce, or even mix it with wasabi if you like spicy food.

Did you know?
Sushi rice is naturally rich in carbohydrates, but it doesn't contain much fibre. The veggies add fibre, vitamins, and minerals.

1

Put the rice in a sieve and rinse it under plenty of cold water until the water runs clear.

2

Put the rice in a pan. Add the cold water and carefully bring to the boil, then cover and simmer for 10 minutes.

3

Leave the rice off the heat for 10 minutes, with the lid still on. Then put it in a shallow dish. Pour on the vinegar and mix.

4

Carefully peel 12 thin, long strips of cucumber. Pat with kitchen paper to remove excess water.

5

Spread the rice evenly down the centre of each strip of cucumber.

Ingredients

125g (4½oz) sushi rice

180ml (6fl oz) cold water

1 tsp white balsamic vinegar

1 large cucumber

For the cream cheese filling

6 tbsp cream cheese

4 tbsp grated carrot, patted dry with kitchen paper

½ red or yellow pepper, diced

1 tbsp raisins or sultanas

sea salt and freshly ground black pepper

1 tbsp dark soy sauce

To make the filling, mix together the cream cheese, carrot, pepper, and raisins. Season well.

Add the MIX!

Spoon on small dollops of the cream cheese mix, then roll the cucumber. Try not to overfill. Serve with the soy sauce in a small bowl for dipping.

Roll it up!

Delicious drinks

Fruity freshness

Start your day with an energy-rich protein shake, whizz up the best-ever mango lassi to serve with a spicy dish, or make a rich hot chocolate to warm up on a cold day. Create impressive fizzy fruity drinks to serve at a party.

Shake and stir!

Fruit and nut
shake

This shake has a secret ingredient – tasty almond butter, which boosts the protein and fibre in this delicious drink.

Did you know?

A tablespoon of almond butter contains about 3 grams of protein. It's also a source of iron, fibre, and heart-healthy fats.

1

Place all the ingredients in a blender or food processor.

Ingredients

150g (5½oz) frozen or fresh mixed berries

1 small banana, chopped

300ml (10fl oz) almond milk or dairy milk

2 tbsp almond butter

2 tbsp porridge oats

small handful of almonds or cashews

2 Blitz until smooth.

Blitz!

You can use other fruits, too!

Swap the berries for your favourites.

Kiwis

3

Your shake is best drunk fresh, but can be kept overnight in the fridge.

Mangoes

Pineapples

Fizzy fruit drinks

These cooling drinks look
fun and taste amazing!

Peach passion

Cucumber cooler

Watermelon fizz

SERVES 4
PREP 10 MINS

SERVES 4
PREP 10 MINS

SERVES 4-6
PREP 10 MINS

Cucumber cooler

½ cucumber, thinly sliced, plus extra to garnish

2 kiwis, peeled and chopped

1 lime, chopped

handful of mint leaves, plus extra to garnish

handful of ice cubes

600ml (1 pint) tonic water

Special equipment

muddler

1

2

Put most of the cucumber in the bottom of the glasses, then add the kiwi, lime, and mint leaves. Muddle (stir and squash) everything to release the flavours.

Add the ice cubes and pour in the tonic water. Garnish with the extra cucumber slices and mint leaves.

Watermelon fizz

1 watermelon, peeled carefully, cut into quarters, deseeded and cut into chunks

2 limes, chopped (reserve a few fine slices, to garnish)

6 tsp sugar

handful of strawberries, roughly chopped (reserve a few slices, to garnish)

handful of ice cubes

500ml (16fl oz) sparkling water or soda water

handful of mint leaves, to garnish

1

2

Whizz the watermelon and limes in a blender until puréed. Tip the sugar onto a plate.

Wet the rim of each glass and place on the sugar to coat the rim. Pour the purée into each glass. Add the strawberries, ice, and water. Garnish with the mint leaves and the slices of lime and reserved strawberry.

Peach passion

a few mint leaves

juice of 1 lime

1 small fresh pineapple, peeled and roughly chopped (reserve a few pieces with skin on, to garnish)

2 peaches, pitted and chopped

handful of crushed ice

900ml (1½ pints) sparkling water

Special equipment

muddler

1

2

Muddle the mint leaves and lime juice in the glasses. Whizz the pineapple in a blender.

Put the pineapple, peaches, ice, and sparkling water in the glasses. Garnish with the reserved peach slices.

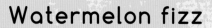

Oat-milk hot chocolate

This delicious oat-milk hot chocolate is the perfect drink for cold days.

Did you know?

Oat milk is naturally low in saturated fat and contains a type of fibre called beta glucan, which helps protect your heart.

1

Put the oat milk and cinnamon stick in a pan, bring almost to the boil, then carefully remove from the heat. Leave to cool for 10 minutes. Remove the cinnamon stick.

Ingredients

250ml (9fl oz) oat milk

1 cinnamon stick

50g (1¾oz) dark chocolate (70% or above), broken into pieces

25g (scant 1oz) milk chocolate, broken into pieces

mini vegan marshmallows, to serve

handful of grated dark chocolate, to serve

2

Add both the chocolates to a heatproof bowl and sit the bowl over a pan of simmering water. Carefully and gently heat until melted, stirring occasionally.

Stir it!

3

Return the pan of milk to the heat and carefully add the melted chocolate. Whisk until combined. Pour into two cups and top with the marshmallows and grated dark chocolate to serve.

Mango
lassi

A super-refreshing, Indian, smoothie-style drink. It's delicious served cold!

SERVES 4
PREP 15 MINS

Did you know?

Yogurt and milk are both rich in calcium, which is important for strong bones. They also provide a good amount of vitamins B2 and B12.

1

Put the mango, milk, and yogurt into a blender and whizz until blended.

Whizz it!

Ingredients

2 mangoes, peeled, pitted and flesh roughly chopped

200ml (7fl oz) milk

300g (10oz) natural yogurt

handful of ice cubes

2 Add the ice cubes and whizz again.

Blitz!

You can use other fruits, too!

Swap the mango for your favourites.

Avocados

Peaches

3

Trickle in a little more milk if the mixture is too thick. Pour into glasses to serve.

Strawberries

83

Moreish
main meals

Stack
it up!

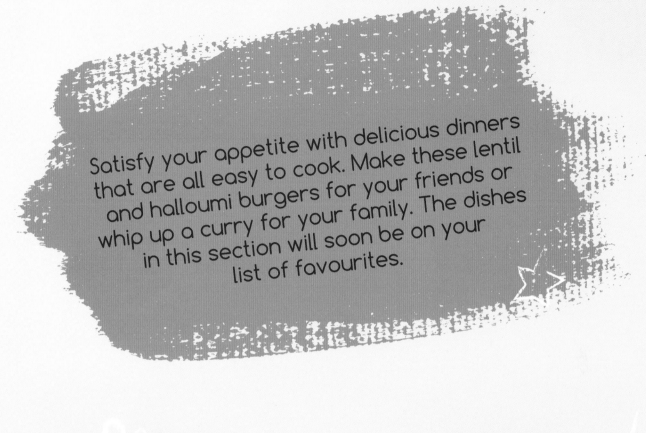

Satisfy your appetite with delicious dinners that are all easy to cook. Make these lentil and halloumi burgers for your friends or whip up a curry for your family. The dishes in this section will soon be on your list of favourites.

Sweet potato lasagne

Instead of pasta, this layered lasagne uses delicious sweet potatoes and is filled with a tasty mix of lentils and mushrooms. It's really good for you, too!

1

Preheat the oven to 200°C (400°F/Gas 6). Put the potato slices in a pan of salted water, carefully bring to the boil, then reduce to a simmer and cook for 3 minutes. Drain well.

2

In a large frying pan, heat the oil over a medium heat. Carefully add the onion and season well, then cook for 2 minutes. Add the garlic and oregano and cook for a few seconds.

3

Stir in the mushrooms and cook for about 5–6 minutes, until they start to soften and become juicy.

4

Tip in the tomatoes, 400ml (14fl oz) boiling water, and the lentils. Carefully bring to the boil, then reduce the heat to a simmer and cook for 15 minutes, until the mixture has thickened.

5

Spoon a third of the lentil mix into an ovenproof dish, cover with a layer of sweet potato, spread with some ricotta. Repeat the layering twice more.

6 Top with the grated cheese, cover with foil, and cook in the oven for an hour. Carefully remove the foil for the last 10 minutes – so the top turns golden and bubbly.

Grate!

87

Green bean
casserole

SERVES 4
PREP 15 MINS
COOK 55 MINS

For this hearty dish, delicious beans, tomatoes, potatoes, and herbs, are all thrown into the pot to meld together and do their magic!

1

Carefully heat the oil in a casserole or large pan over a medium heat. Add the onion, season well, and cook for 2 minutes. Add the garlic and cook for another minute, then stir in the paprika.

2

Add the potatoes, tomatoes, and beans. Mix well together.

Toss it all together!

3

Carefully pour in the stock, bring it to the boil, then reduce it to a simmer. Put a lid on and cook for 45 minutes, until the vegetables are tender.

4

Add the peas, dill, and some more seasoning. Cook for 5 minutes. Carefully transfer to a serving dish and keep hot.

Ingredients

1 tbsp olive oil

1 onion, finely chopped

pinch of sea salt and freshly ground black pepper

2 garlic cloves, finely chopped

2 tsp paprika

250g (9oz) baby new potatoes, larger ones halved

large handful of cherry tomatoes

200g (7oz) green beans, trimmed and halved

1 vegetable stock cube, dissolved in 750ml (1¼ pints) hot water

handful of frozen peas, defrosted

handful of dill, chopped

250g (9oz) brown rice, to serve

5

Carefully boil the brown rice until tender, or follow the pack instructions. Drain and serve with the casserole.

Did you know?

This meal is high in fibre and provides a good variety of vitamins and minerals. To boost the protein content, serve it with grated cheese.

Sweet potato
falafel balls

MAKES 30
PREP 15 MNS
COOK 50 MINS

Falafel is a Middle Eastern snack that is now popular all over the world. It will soon be a favourite of yours, too.

yogurt and mint dip

pitta bread

Did you know?
One small sweet potato provides over half your recommended amount of vitamin A, which is important for healthy skin and eyes.

1

Preheat the oven to 200°C (400°F/Gas 6). Prick the sweet potato and place on a baking tray. Bake for 40 minutes. Allow to cool slightly. Leave the oven on.

Ingredients

1 medium sweet potato, about 250g (9oz)

420g (15½oz) can chickpeas, rinsed and drained

1 garlic clove, crushed

1 tsp ground cumin

2 tsp ground coriander

1 tsp smoked paprika

2 tbsp chopped flat-leaf parsley

1 tsp salt

1 tsp freshly ground black pepper

1 tsp baking powder

2 tsp lemon juice

2 tbsp plain flour

4 tbsp sesame seeds

pitta bread, to serve

green salad, to serve

For the yogurt and mint dip

100g (3½oz) low-fat natural yogurt

2 tbsp chopped fresh mint

¼ cucumber, finely chopped

2

chickpeas

ground cumin

smoked paprika

flat-leaf parsley

Place the chickpeas, garlic, spices, parsley, and seasoning in a food processor. Pulse until coarsely chopped.

3

Remove the skin and roughly chop the cooked potato. Add to the food processor with the baking powder, lemon juice, and flour. Pulse until combined.

4

Shape the mixture into around 30 balls. Coat the balls in sesame seeds and bake in the hot oven for 10 minutes.

sesame seeds

5

Mix it!

yogurt

cucumber

fresh mint

Mix the ingredients for the dip. Serve the falafel with warmed pitta, salad, and dip.

Pizza
dough

MAKES 4 PIZZAS
PREP 20 MINS
RISE 1½ HRS

Once you have mastered this simple pizza dough and made some pizza sauce, go to page 94 and choose a tasty topping!

Ingredients

500g (1lb 2oz) strong white bread flour, plus extra for dusting

pinch of sea salt

7g (¼oz) sachet dried yeast

3 tbsp olive oil, plus extra for greasing

1

Put the flour, salt, and yeast into the bowl of a food mixer. Attach the dough hook and mix on slow speed. Add the oil and slowly pour in 300ml (10fl oz) lukewarm water.

2

Keep mixing slowly until the dough comes together. Turn the mixer to a higher speed and mix for 5 minutes, until it forms a ball and slaps against the sides of the bowl.

3

On a lightly floured surface, knead the dough, stretching and pulling as you go. Add flour if sticky, but don't make the dough too dry. Knead for about 10 minutes or until the dough starts to feel smooth and springy.

4

Lightly grease a bowl with olive oil, then add the dough. Cover with cling film and put the bowl in a warm place. Leave it to prove for about 1 hour, or until doubled in size.

5

Knock the dough down by lightly punching it, tip it out onto a floured surface, and cut into four pieces. Cover with cling film and leave for 30 minutes, until doubled in size. Then roll each piece out into a circle.

Once you've made your pizza dough into a ball and allowed it to fully rise (Step 4), you can freeze it. Wrap well in cling film and keep in the freezer for up to one month. When ready to use, defrost in the fridge overnight, then put it in a warm place for an hour to double in size again, before moving on to Step 5.

To make tomato pizza sauce, carefully heat 1 tablespoon olive oil in a large frying pan over a medium heat. Add 1 onion, finely chopped, and 2 garlic cloves, finely chopped. Season well, then cook for 2 minutes.

Add 2 x 400g (14oz) cans plum tomatoes, cook for 5 minutes, and crush the tomatoes using the back of a wooden spoon. Stir in 2 teaspoons tomato purée and simmer for 10–15 minutes, until the sauce starts to thicken. Add a pinch of dried oregano if you wish.

Three ways
with pizza

Now that you've made your pizza dough
and tomato sauce, it's time to top it off
with some delicious veggies!

To prepare a pizza base, put
one ball of dough on a lightly
floured surface and roll
it gently with a rolling pin,
rotating as you go; it will keep
pinging back. Continue to roll
and stretch the dough until
you have a large, round circle.

Pizza bianca

Preheat the oven to 220°C (425°F/Gas 7). Put the
spinach in a bowl, cover with cling film, and
microwave for 1–2 minutes until it wilts. Allow to cool
and then squeeze out the water. Carefully put a
pizza base on a hot baking sheet, brush with olive
oil, sprinkle with sea salt, and top with the spinach,
leaving a 2cm (¾in) edge all around. Scatter with
garlic slices and ricotta. Drizzle with a little more
oil, then sprinkle with black pepper and chilli flakes
(if using). Cook in the oven for 10–15 minutes,
until the edge of the base is crispy and the top
is bubbling.

Mushrooms and courgette ribbons

Preheat the oven to 220°C (425°F/Gas 7). Carefully put a pizza base on a hot baking sheet and spread with tomato sauce, leaving a 2cm (¾in) edge all around. Add the courgette ribbons and mushrooms, then scatter over the grated cheese. Top with a drizzle of oil and a sprinkling of black pepper. Cook in the oven for 10–15 minutes, until the base is crispy and the top is bubbling.

Pesto and sun-dried tomatoes

Preheat the oven to 220°C (425°F/Gas 7). Carefully put a pizza base on a hot baking sheet and spread with tomato sauce, leaving a 2cm (¾in) edge all around. Spoon dollops of pesto on top, then scatter with the sun-dried tomatoes and mozzarella. Add a sprinkling of olive oil and the black pepper. Cook in the oven for 10–15 minutes, until the base is crispy and the top is bubbling.

Ingredients

Pizza bianca (to top 1 pizza)

2 large handfuls of spinach leaves

extra virgin olive oil, plus extra for topping

pinch of sea salt

2 garlic cloves, thinly sliced

3–4 tbsp ricotta cheese

freshly ground black pepper

sprinkle of chilli flakes (optional)

Pesto and sun-dried tomatoes (to top 1 pizza)

3 tbsp tomato sauce

2 tbsp pesto

6 sun-dried tomatoes, chopped

½ ball mozzarella, torn into small pieces

extra virgin olive oil

freshly grated black pepper

Mushrooms and courgette ribbons (to top 1 pizza)

3 tbsp tomato sauce

1 medium courgette, thinly sliced into ribbon strips with a peeler

handful of mushrooms, thinly sliced

125g (4½oz) grated hard cheese, or use mozzarella if you prefer

extra virgin olive oil

freshly ground black pepper

Calzone pizza

MAKES 4
PREP 20 MINS
RISE 2$^1/_2$ HRS
COOK 20 MINS

A calzone is a folded pizza which is stuffed with a delicious filling. It's important not to over-fill or it will ooze out.

Ingredients

1 tbsp olive oil, plus extra for greasing

200g (7oz) mushrooms, sliced

pinch of sea salt and freshly ground black pepper

300g (10oz) spinach leaves, torn

4 tbsp passata

200g (7oz) mozzarella

salad leaves, to serve

For the dough

500g (1lb 2oz) strong white bread flour, plus extra for dusting

7g (¼oz) sachet dried yeast

pinch of sea salt

1 tbsp olive oil

1

For the dough, put the flour, yeast, and salt into the bowl of a food mixer. Mix using the dough hook. Add 325ml (11fl oz) warm water and the oil. Mix for 10 minutes, until the dough begins to slap against the sides of the bowl.

2

Using floured hands, scoop the dough out of the bowl and put it onto a lightly floured surface. Knead for 5 minutes.

3

Lightly grease a clean bowl. Put the dough in it and cover with cling film. Leave the dough to rise in a warm place for 2 hours or until doubled in size. Preheat the oven to 200°C (400°F/Gas 6).

4

Knock the air out of the dough by lightly punching it. Tip it out of the bowl onto a lightly floured surface. Knead for 1 minute, then divide into four balls. Place them on a baking sheet and put in a warm place to rise for 30 minutes.

5

Carefully heat the olive oil in a large frying pan over a medium heat, then add the mushrooms and season well. Cook for 2 minutes until the mushrooms are soft. Stir in the spinach.

6

Put a baking sheet in the oven to get hot. Roll the dough balls out to about 20cm (8in) rounds. Spread passata over the dough circles, leaving a 2cm (¾in) edge all around.

7

Put some mushroom and spinach mixture on half of each round. Sprinkle over the mozzarella. Wet the edge with water, then fold over. Pinch the edges to seal. Carefully place on baking sheets and bake in the oven for 20 minutes. Do this in two batches. Serve with the salad leaves.

Spread it!

Veggie sausages and mashed potatoes

It is really satisfying and fun to make your own veggie sausages for dinner. Serve with creamy mash, tasty greens, and warm vegetarian gravy.

SERVES 6
PREP 15 MINS
CHILL 50 MINS
COOK 50 MINS

Did you know?

This meal provides plenty of protein from the lentils, nuts, and eggs as well as carbs from the potatoes and breadcrumbs. All you need to add is a green veg to make a healthy balanced meal.

1

Soak the mushrooms in a bowl of hot water for 20 minutes. Carefully remove using a slotted spoon and chop. Reserve the soaking water.

2

Heat half a tablespoon of the oil in a large frying pan over a medium heat. Add the onion. Season well. Cook for 3 minutes. Stir in the garlic and cook for another minute.

3

Use a food processor to whizz the mushrooms, lentils, nuts, apple, breadcrumbs, herbs, tomato purée, onion, and garlic into a coarse mixture.

Ingredients

15g (½oz) dried porcini mushrooms

3 tbsp olive oil, for frying

1 onion, finely chopped

sea salt and freshly ground black pepper

2 garlic cloves, finely chopped

2 x 420g (15½oz) cans green lentils, rinsed and drained

200g (7oz) ground pecan nuts or walnuts

1 apple, grated

250g (9oz) fresh breadcrumbs

handful of thyme leaves

handful of flat-leaf parsley, finely chopped

½ tbsp tomato purée

2 eggs

4 tsp vegetarian gravy granules, dissolved in 280ml (9½fl oz) boiling water, to serve

300g (10oz) broccoli, steamed, to serve

For the mash

500g (1lb 2oz) potatoes, peeled and chopped

25g (scant 1oz) butter

150ml (5fl oz) milk

4

Crack in one egg at a time. Whizz again. Add a little of the reserved mushroom soaking water. Season well. Put the mixture into a bowl. Chill for 30 minutes.

5

Shape the chilled mixture into 10–12 balls. Squish them, then roll them into sausage shapes. Put them on a plate or baking sheet. Chill for 20 minutes.

6

Over a medium heat, carefully fry the sausages in the remaining oil, until golden, turning them regularly. Boil the potatoes, until soft. Drain and then mash. Stir in the butter and milk and season.

Mash it!

Cauliflower
steaks

This is such a clever and tasty way to cook cauliflower – it is so delicious, you'll end up eating lots of this healthy veg.

Did you know?

Cauliflower is a good source of vitamin K, which will help keep your bones healthy and strong.

Ingredients

2 large whole cauliflowers, outer leaves removed

3 tbsp olive oil

sea salt and freshly ground black pepper

2 tsp turmeric

grated zest of 1 lemon

1 red chilli, deseeded and finely chopped

handful of flat-leaf parsley, leaves only, finely chopped

3 tsp capers, chopped

6 potatoes, peeled and cubed, to serve

2–3 rosemary stalks, leaves removed, to serve

Chop!

1

Sit the cauliflowers on a board with the stems facing up, then carefully slice vertically into even sized steaks. You should get 3–4 per cauliflower. Use all the smaller pieces around the edges too.

2

Mix 2 tablespoons of the oil, some seasoning, the turmeric, lemon zest, and half the chilli in a medium bowl. Use a pastry brush to coat all of the cauliflower steaks with the mixture.

3

Heat a griddle pan to hot then add the cauliflower, in batches. Carefully cook the steaks for 4–5 minutes, then turn over and cook for another 4–5 minutes or until the cauliflower is charred and just tender.

4

Put the steaks on serving plates, and scatter over parsley, capers, and the remaining chilli before serving.

Serve with...

Preheat the oven to 200°C (400°F/Gas 6). Put the potatoes and rosemary in a large roasting tin. Drizzle over the remaining oil and season well. Use your hands to help coat the potatoes and to spread them out in the tin. Roast for 25–30 minutes or until tender.

Broccoli and bean
stir-fry

This tasty dish is really easy to make and is perfect for a quick dinner when you have lots on.

SERVES 4
PREP 10 MINS
COOK 25 MINS

Did you know?

Broccoli and tomatoes are both rich in vitamin C, which will help your body absorb the iron from the beans.

Ingredients

1 head broccoli, cut into florets

200g (7oz) fine green beans, trimmed and chopped into thirds

1 tbsp sesame oil

bunch of spring onions, trimmed and thinly sliced (reserve some of the green ends for topping)

2 garlic cloves, thinly sliced

1 red chilli, halved, deseeded and thinly sliced

1 tbsp fresh ginger, peeled and thinly sliced

400g (14oz) can kidney beans, rinsed and drained

handful of cherry tomatoes

300g (10oz) straight-to-wok medium noodles

10g (¼oz) black or white sesame seeds, or a mixture of both

handful of coriander leaves (optional)

For the sauce

3 tbsp lime juice

2 tbsp light soy sauce, plus extra if needed

2 tsp caster sugar

2 tsp cornflour

Mix it!

Put the sauce ingredients into a small bowl and whisk together, ready to add to the wok.

1

Carefully put the broccoli in a large pan of boiling, salted water and cook for 5 minutes. Add the green beans for the last 3 minutes. Carefully drain, using a colander, then tip the vegetables into a bowl of cold water. Drain again when ready to use.

3

2

Carefully heat the sesame oil in a large wok, over a high heat. Take care near hot oil and a hot wok. Add the white spring onion and some of the greens and cook for 1 minute. Add the garlic, chilli, and ginger and cook for another minute. Stir continuously, so the stir-fry doesn't burn.

Add the drained broccoli and green beans to the wok. Tip in the kidney beans and tomatoes. Stir and cook for 2 minutes. Add the sauce mixture (see below) and let it bubble for 2 minutes, stirring continuously.

4

Stir in the noodles, so they get really well coated and heated through. Sprinkle with remaining green spring onion, sesame seeds, and coriander leaves, if using. Serve while piping hot.

103

Chickpea and sweet potato **curry**

This isn't a hot curry, although you could ramp it up with more chillies if you like – it's a lovely jumble of flavours and colours.

SERVES 4
PREP 10 MINS
COOK 50 MINS

Ingredients

1 tbsp olive oil

1 red onion, roughly chopped

sea salt and freshly ground black pepper

2 garlic cloves, finely chopped

1 red chilli, deseeded and finely chopped

1 tbsp fresh ginger, grated

2 tsp garam masala

2 sweet potatoes, peeled and cubed

400g (14oz) can chickpeas, rinsed and drained

400g (14oz) can chopped tomatoes

400g (14oz) can coconut milk

300g (10oz) spinach leaves

bunch of coriander, chopped

200g (7oz) brown basmati rice, to serve

For the salad

1 tomato, roughly chopped

½ cucumber, roughly chopped

½ red onion, roughly chopped

handful of coriander leaves, chopped

1 Carefully heat the oil in a large pan over a medium heat, and add the onion. Season well and cook for 2–3 minutes until soft. Stir in the garlic, chilli, ginger, and garam masala, and cook for another minute more. Add the sweet potatoes and stir.

2 Carefully tip in the chickpeas, tomatoes, and coconut milk and bring to the boil. Then reduce to a simmer and cook gently for 15 minutes, until the potatoes are tender.

3 Add the spinach leaves in small amounts at a time, stir, and cook until they wilt. Then stir in the coriander.

Serve with...

Put the rice in a sieve and rinse. Bring 400ml (14fl oz) of water to the boil in a large pan. Carefully tip the rice into the boiling water. Cook for 25–30 minutes, or until tender. All the water should be absorbed by the rice. In a small bowl, mix the ingredients together for the side salad.

Coconut rice with spicy beans

These colourful veggies look great and taste amazing. It's a really quick supper to make.

SERVES 4
PREP 10 MINS
COOK 20 MINS

spicy!

To make this dish vegan, swap the honey for maple syrup.

1

Carefully heat the sesame oil in a large frying pan, over a medium heat. Add the spring onions and peppers, and stir around the pan for 3 minutes. Add the ginger, chilli, chilli flakes, and lime zest.

2

Stir in the lime juice, soy sauce mix, and season with black pepper. Cook, stirring for 2 minutes.

Stir it well.

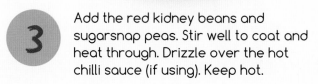

3

Add the red kidney beans and sugarsnap peas. Stir well to coat and heat through. Drizzle over the hot chilli sauce (if using). Keep hot.

Ingredients

1 tbsp sesame oil

bunch of spring onions, thinly sliced

2 red peppers, halved, deseeded and roughly chopped

1 tbsp fresh ginger, grated

1 red chilli, thinly sliced

sprinkle of chilli flakes

grated zest and juice of 1 lime

2 tbsp dark soy sauce, mixed with 2 tsp runny honey

freshly ground black pepper

400g (14oz) can red kidney beans, rinsed and drained

handful of sugarsnap peas, sliced diagonally

hot chilli sauce, to serve (optional)

200g (7oz) basmati rice, rinsed

200ml (7fl oz) coconut milk

4

Put the rice in a saucepan and tip in the coconut milk and 200ml (7fl oz) water. Add a pinch of salt and carefully bring to the boil, then cover with a lid and reduce to a simmer. Cook for 15 minutes, until the rice is tender and the liquid has been absorbed. Serve with the spicy beans.

Veggie goulash with herby dumplings

Spiced with sweet paprika and packed with delicious vegetables, this veggie goulash is made extra special with the herby dumplings.

Ingredients

1 tbsp olive oil

1 onion, finely chopped

sea salt and freshly ground black pepper

2 garlic cloves, finely chopped

4 carrots, peeled and diced

2 red peppers, halved, deseeded and roughly chopped

4 potatoes, peeled and cut into chunks

4 tomatoes, roughly chopped

1 tbsp sweet paprika

400g (14oz) can mixed beans or butter beans, rinsed and drained

1 vegetable stock cube, dissolved in 750ml (1¼ pints) hot water

few sprigs of flat-leaf parsley, finely chopped

For the dumplings

100g (3½oz) self-raising flour

pinch of sea salt

50g (1¾oz) butter, cubed

a few chives, snipped

SERVES 6
PREP 20 MINS
COOK 1½ HRS

1

Preheat the oven to 200°C (400°F/Gas 6). Carefully heat the oil in a large casserole dish over a medium heat and add the onion. Season well. Cook for 2 minutes, then stir through the garlic and carrots. Cook for a few more minutes.

2

Add the peppers and potatoes. Cook for 5 minutes, stirring everything around the pan. Stir in the tomatoes and paprika.

3

Stir in the beans, carefully add the vegetable stock and bring to the boil. Put the lid on and cook in the oven for 1 hour 20 minutes. Check to make sure it isn't drying out. If it is, top it up with a little hot water.

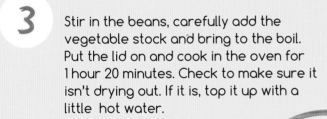

4

While the goulash is cooking, make the dumplings. Put the flour and sea salt into a bowl, mix together, then add the butter. Using your fingertips, rub in the butter until the mixture looks like breadcrumbs.

5

Stir in the chives, then slowly trickle in 2 teaspoons of water and bring the mixture together using your hands. Trickle in a few more drops of water if the mixture is too dry.

6

Roll the mixture into 12 even-sized balls. Add them to the casserole dish 20 minutes before the end of cooking. Carefully remove the goulash from the oven, sprinkle with the chopped parsley, and serve.

This is delicious eaten with some warmed crusty bread.

Lentil burgers
with halloumi

Stuffed with halloumi, carrot, and beetroot, these juicy burgers are irresistible!

Did you know?
A good source of protein, 50g (1¾oz) of cooked lentils will also count as a serving of vegetables.

MAKES 8
PREP 20 MINS
CHILL 20 MINS
COOK 30 MINS

1

Put the lentils in a large mixing bowl, then add the onion, garlic, and chilli flakes. Season well and mix together.

Ingredients

2 x 400g (14oz) cans brown lentils, rinsed and drained

1 red onion, finely chopped

2 garlic cloves, finely chopped

sprinkle of chilli flakes

sea salt and freshly ground black pepper

2 carrots, peeled and grated

1 raw beetroot, peeled and grated

125g (4½oz) halloumi, grated

125g (4½oz) white breadcrumbs

handful of flat-leaf parsley, chopped

2 eggs

8 brioche buns, to serve

8 lettuce leaves, to serve

16 slices of tomato, to serve

8 slices of gherkin (optional), to serve

tomato sauce, to serve

2

Add the grated carrot and beetroot and stir well.

3

Stir in the halloumi, breadcrumbs, and parsley.

4

Add the eggs and mix well. Using your hands, squish it all together until the mixture starts to bind. With wet hands, scoop out eight even-sized balls of mixture.

5

Put the balls on a lined baking sheet and gently press down. Cover with cling film and chill in the fridge for 20 minutes to firm up. Preheat the oven to 200°C (400°F/Gas 6).

6

Cook in the oven for 15–20 minutes until cooked through. Serve in a bun, sandwiched with lettuce, tomato, and gherkin (if using), and a squeeze of sauce, if you wish.

Sweet stuff

Rich and moist!

These tempting treats contain fruit and veg that add delicious flavouring and texture. Roll up chocolate energy balls, mix together tasty orange cookies, whizz up homemade avocado ice cream, then bake beetroot brownies and zingy lime pie.

Almond, chocolate, and coconut
energy balls

These are so easy to make and require no cooking: just blitz, roll, and chill! They give you instant energy when hunger strikes.

MAKES 12
PREP 15 MINS
CHILL 20 MINS
OR **OVERNIGHT**

Mix it!

raisins

cocoa powder

runny honey

desiccated coconut

hot water

Ingredients

85g (3oz) whole almonds, skin on

20g (¾oz) dark chocolate cocoa powder

85g (3oz) raisins

30g (1oz) desiccated coconut

1 tsp runny honey

60g (2oz) desiccated coconut, to roll the balls in

1 Put the almonds in a food processor and whizz until finely chopped. Add the cocoa, raisins, and the 30g (1oz) coconut and whizz again. Add the honey and carefully pour in about 2 tablespoons hot (not boiling) water. Blitz until the mixture comes together.

ROLL IT UP!

2

Try this!
Swap the honey with maple syrup or agave nectar to make these energy balls vegan.

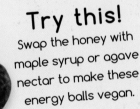

Roll the mixture into 12 balls. Put the 60g (2oz) of coconut in a small bowl. Roll half of the balls in the coconut. Put all the balls on a baking tray lined with greaseproof paper. Chill for 20 minutes or overnight.

3 Put the balls in an airtight container and eat them when you fancy an energy boost. Alternatively, give them away in a gift box.

Avocado and banana
ice cream

Surprise your friends with this non-dairy ice cream, which is created without an ice cream maker.

MAKES 1 LITRE, PREP 15 MINS PLUS CHURNING AND FREEZING TIME

1

In a food processor, add the coconut milk, avocados, banana, matcha tea, lime juice, maple syrup, and peppermint extract. Whizz until blended and smooth. Taste for sweetness and stir in more maple syrup if needed.

2

Transfer to a freezer-proof container and put it in the freezer for about 1 hour.

3

Take it out of the freezer and put it back in the food processor. Whizz again until smooth. Put it back into the container and place back in the freezer.

4

Take it out and whizz again after 20 minutes, so it doesn't get too frozen. This helps to avoid it becoming crystallised and to remain creamy. Do this a couple more times, so it becomes nice and thick.

5

On the last time in the food processor, blend then stir in the chocolate chips. Put back into the container, then into the freezer. Serve when frozen.

Ingredients

2 x 400g (14oz) cans coconut milk

3 ripe avocados, pitted

2 ripe bananas

½ tsp matcha green tea powder

juice of 1 lime (to prevent discoloration)

3 tbsp maple syrup

2 drops of peppermint extract

75g (2½oz) vegan dark chocolate chips (70% cocoa) or chocolate broken into small pieces

Orange and chocolate
cookies

When you get the hang of this easy dough mix, you can become more adventurous and add your favourite spices or flavoured chocolate.

SERVES 8
PREP 20 MINS
COOK 10 MINS

1

Preheat the oven to 180°C (350°F/Gas 4). Grease 2 baking trays. Put the flour into a large bowl, add the butter and rub it in using your fingertips until the mixture looks like breadcrumbs.

2

Stir it!

Grate it!

Tip in the sugar and rub it in. Stir in the orange zest and the white chocolate chips.

3

Using your hands, bring the dough together. Use a little more flour if the dough is too wet. Halve the dough and roll both halves into a sausage shape. Carefully cut each shape into 8 pieces.

4

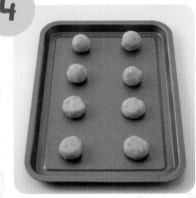

Roll the dough pieces into 16 balls. Put them onto the greased baking trays and gently press down on each one. Bake in the oven for 10 minutes, or until golden.

Ingredients

125g (4½oz) self-raising flour

100g (3½oz) unsalted butter, chilled, and cut into small cubes, plus extra for greasing

50g (1¾oz) caster sugar

grated zest of 1 orange

60g (2oz) white chocolate chips

5

Leave on the tray to cool a little, then carefully transfer the cookies to a wire rack to fully cool.

Cool it!

Beetroot brownies

These are good and squidgy, as brownies should be – the grated beetroot keeps them moist and makes them a little bit healthier.

MAKES 12
PREP 20 MINS
COOK 1 HOUR

Top tip
Put the brownies in an airtight container and they will last you for 3–4 days.

Preheat the oven to 180°C (350°F/Gas 4). Carefully add the beetroot to a pan of boiling water. Then reduce the heat to a simmer and cook with the lid on for 30–35 minutes, until tender. Drain well. When cool enough to handle, peel, grate and set aside.

2

In a heatproof bowl, add the chocolate and butter, sit the bowl over a pan of simmering water, and carefully heat until melted. Stir as it's heated. Remove from the heat and set aside.

3

Add the sugar and eggs to a bowl and whisk until well combined, then mix it with the chocolate.

Ingredients

250g (9oz) raw beetroot

200g (7oz) dark chocolate, broken into even pieces

200g (7oz) unsalted butter, cubed, plus extra for greasing

200g (7oz) golden caster sugar

3 eggs

150g (5½oz) self-raising flour

50g (1¾oz) dark chocolate cocoa powder

Special equipment

22cm (8in) square baking tin, 3–4cm (1½in) deep, greased

4

Stir in the flour and cocoa, then stir in the grated beetroot until it is all mixed in.

5

Pour the mixture into the tray, smooth the top, and bake for 25 minutes. Poke a skewer into it to test that it is cooked. The skewer will be clean if the brownies are cooked. Carefully remove from the oven and leave in the tin to cool, then remove and slice into squares.

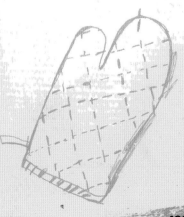

Zingy lime **pie**

This delicious dessert is fun to make. It's sweet, sour, and crunchy!

SERVES 6
PREP 20 MINS
COOK 25 MINS
PLUS CHILLING

1

Preheat the oven to 180°C (350°F/Gas 4). Whizz the biscuits in a food processor until they look like breadcrumbs. Melt the butter in a saucepan. Tip the biscuits into the butter and mix well.

Mix it!

Ingredients

200g (7oz) ginger biscuits or digestive biscuits

50g (1¾oz) unsalted butter

For the filling

3 large egg yolks

grated zest of 2 limes and juice of 4 limes

400ml (14fl oz) condensed milk

200ml (7fl oz) double cream, for the topping

Special equipment

22cm (8½in) fluted pie dish

icing piping bag

* Please note: the finished recipe contains egg that isn't fully cooked.

2

3

4

Pour the filling over the biscuit base, smooth the top, and bake for 15 minutes, or until just set. Remove from the oven and leave to cool completely. Chill in the fridge until ready serve.

Tip into the pie dish, spread out well, and press firmly into the base and sides. Bake in the oven for 10 minutes until firm. Take it out and leave to cool.

In a large bowl, whisk the egg yolks for 1 minute, then add the lime zest, juice, and the condensed milk. Whisk again until well combined.

5

To decorate, whisk the cream in a bowl until it just starts to make soft peaks. Put the cream in the piping bag and pipe around the edges of the pie.

Decorate it!

Nutritional
information

Look here to find out what's in your food. The numbers don't include extras or variations suggested in the recipes. Remember to eat a balanced diet. Calories measure the energy value of a food when it is eaten and digested.

Brilliant breakfasts

Avocado mash on sourdough toast
- Calories 457
- Fat 23g
- Saturated Fat 4.5g
- Protein 10.5g
- Fibre 7g
- Salt 1.3g

Crunchy, sweet pancakes
- Calories 132
- Fat 4g
- Saturated Fat 1g
- Protein 4g
- Fibre 1g
- Salt 0.4g

Scrambled eggs
- Calories 285
- Fat 27g
- Saturated Fat 15g
- Protein 9g
- Fibre 0g
- Salt 1.2g

Bircher muesli
- Calories 358
- Fat 12g
- Saturated Fat 4g
- Protein 10g
- Fibre 5g
- Salt 0.2g

Mango yogurt with toast dippers
- Calories 392
- Fat 15.5g
- Saturated Fat 9g
- Protein 10g
- Fibre 5g
- Salt 0.5g

Poached eggs with greens and hollandaise sauce
- Calories 755
- Fat 64g
- Saturated Fat 35g
- Protein 18g
- Fibre 4.5g
- Salt 2.3g

Super snacks

Flatbreads and dips
- Calories 556
- Fat 35g
- Saturated Fat 6g
- Protein 16g
- Fibre 8g
- Salt 1.3g

Plantain chips and dips
- Calories 322
- Fat 24g
- Saturated Fat 5g
- Protein 4g
- Fibre 1g
- Salt 0.9g

Warm and fruity bulgur wheat salad
- Calories 543
- Fat 16.5g
- Saturated Fat 2.5g
- Protein 16g
- Fibre 10g
- Salt 0.3g

Chinese rolls (per roll)
- Calories 50
- Fat 0.5g
- Saturated Fat 0g
- Protein 1.5g
- Fibre 0.5g
- Salt 0.6g

Crudités and dips
- Calories 303
- Fat 21.5g
- Saturated Fat 14g
- Protein 11g
- Fibre 3.5g
- Salt 1.5g

Homemade nachos
- Calories 657
- Fat 30g
- Saturated Fat 14g
- Protein 23g
- Fibre 8.5g
- Salt 1.8g

Cheese and herb muffins
- Calories 158
- Fat 9g
- Saturated Fat 5g
- Protein 7g
- Fibre 0.5g
- Salt 0.6g

Watermelon and feta summer salad
- Calories 341
- Fat 16g
- Saturated Fat 6g
- Protein 14.5g
- Fibre 3.5g
- Salt 0.9g

Parsnip and sweet potato fries
- Calories 224
- Fat 7g
- Saturated Fat 1g
- Protein 3g
- Fibre 8g
- Salt 0.4g

Lovely lunches

Pumpkin soup
- Calories 230
- Fat 6.5g
- Saturated Fat 1.5g
- Protein 8g
- Fibre 5g
- Salt 0.7g

Vegetable wraps
- Calories 592
- Fat 38g
- Saturated Fat 14g
- Protein 18g
- Fibre 6g
- Salt 2.9g

Vegetable frittata
- Calories 256
- Fat 16g
- Saturated Fat 5.5g
- Protein 17g
- Fibre 3g
- Salt 0.9g

Pearl barley risotto
- Calories 521
- Fat 14g
- Saturated Fat 3g
- Protein 13.5g
- Fibre 5g
- Salt 0.6g

Pasta and homemade pesto
- Calories 826
- Fat 51g
- Saturated Fat 10.5g
- Protein 21g
- Fibre 4g
- Salt 0.4g

Quesadillas
- Calories 579
- Fat 16g
- Saturated Fat 4.5g
- Protein 15g
- Fibre 9g
- Salt 1.3g

Lentil dhal and paratha bread
- Calories 580
- Fat 16g
- Saturated Fat 1.5g
- Protein 21g
- Fibre 7.5g
- Salt 0.6g

Veggie gyoza (per gyoza)
- Calories 66
- Fat 0.5g
- Saturated Fat 0.1g
- Protein 2g
- Fibre 0.1g
- Salt 0.4g

Easy veggie rolls (per roll)
- Calories 67
- Fat 2g
- Saturated Fat 1g
- Protein 1.5g
- Fibre 0.7g
- Salt 0.25g

Delicious drinks

Fruit and nut shake (2 servings)
- Calories 337
- Fat 20g
- Saturated Fat 2g
- Protein 10g
- Fibre 4.5g
- Salt 0.2g

Peach passion
- Calories 100
- Fat 0g
- Saturated Fat 0g
- Protein 0g
- Fibre 3g
- Salt 0g

Cucumber cooler
- Calories 55
- Fat 0g
- Saturated Fat 0g
- Protein 0.5g
- Fibre 1g
- Salt 0g

Oat-milk hot chocolate
- Calories 371
- Fat 18.5g
- Saturated Fat 9.5g
- Protein 4g
- Fibre 3.5g
- Salt 0.3g

Watermelon fizz
- Calories 97
- Fat 0g
- Saturated Fat 0g
- Protein 0g
- Fibre 0g
- Salt 0g

Mango lassi
- Calories 134
- Fat 4g
- Saturated Fat 3g
- Protein 6.5g
- Fibre 2g
- Salt 0.2g

Sweet potato lasagne

- Calories 450
- Fat 15g
- Saturated Fat 8g
- Protein 18g
- Fibre 9g
- Salt 0.9g

Green bean casserole

- Calories 350
- Fat 6g
- Saturated Fat 1g
- Protein 10g
- Fibre 5g
- Salt 0.3g

Sweet potato falafel balls

- Calories 300
- Fat 15.5g
- Saturated Fat 2.5g
- Protein 10g
- Fibre 6.5g
- Salt 1.6g

Mushroom and courgette ribbons pizza

- Calories 1999
- Fat 68g
- Saturated Fat 31g
- Protein 50g
- Fibre 5.5g
- Salt 3.5g

Main meals

Pizza bianca

- Calories 800
- Fat 31g
- Saturated Fat 8g
- Protein 25g
- Fibre 6.5g
- Salt 2.2g

Pesto and sun-dried tomatoes pizza

- Calories 1134
- Fat 60g
- Saturated Fat 20g
- Protein 41g
- Fibre 5g
- Salt 2.9g

Calzone pizza

- Calories 640
- Fat 18g
- Saturated Fat 8.5g
- Protein 24g
- Fibre 6g
- Salt 1.1g

Veggie sausages and mashed potatoes

- Calories 325
- Fat 21.5g
- Saturated Fat 3.5g
- Protein 10g
- Fibre 4g
- Salt 0.2g

Cauliflower steaks

- Calories 427
- Fat 10g
- Saturated Fat 1.5g
- Protein 15g
- Fibre 9g
- Salt 0.6g

Broccoli and bean stir-fry

- Calories 269
- Fat 7g
- Saturated Fat 1g
- Protein 10.5g
- Fibre 7g
- Salt 1.3g

Chickpea and sweet potato curry

- Calories 395
- Fat 21g
- Saturated Fat 15g
- Protein 11g
- Fibre 8g
- Salt 0.4g

Coconut rice with spicy beans

- Calories 388
- Fat 12g
- Saturated Fat 8g
- Protein 10g
- Fibre 6g
- Salt 1g

Veggie goulash with herby dumplings

- Calories 350
- Fat 10.5g
- Saturated Fat 5g
- Protein 9g
- Fibre 6g
- Salt 0.6g

Lentil burgers with halloumi

- Calories 367
- Fat 8g
- Saturated Fat 3g
- Protein 17g
- Fibre 7g
- Salt 1.5g

Sweet stuff

Almond, chocolate, and coconut energy balls

- Calories 96
- Fat 7g
- Saturated Fat 3g
- Protein 2g
- Fibre 1.5g
- Salt 0g

Avocado and banana ice cream, per 100ml (3½fl oz)

- Calories 225
- Fat 19g
- Satura ted Fat 13.5g
- Protein 2g
- Fibre 1g
- Salt 0g

Orange and chocolate cookies

- Calories 189
- Fat 11.5g
- Saturated Fat 7g
- Protein 2g
- Fibre 0.5g
- Salt 0.15g

Beetroot brownies

- Calories 345
- Fat 19.5g
- Saturated Fat 12g
- Protein 5g
- Fibre 1.5g
- Salt 0.22g

Zingy lime pie

- Calories 630
- Fat 40g
- Saturated Fat 22g
- Protein 9g
- Fibre 0.5g
- Salt 0.7g

Glossary

amino acids organic molecules used by living organisms to make proteins.

aromatic a pleasant or spicy smell.

batter a thin liquid used to make light cakes and pancakes.

beat stirring or mixing quickly until smooth, using a whisk, spoon, or mixer.

blend mixing ingredients together in a blender or food processor until combined.

boil heating liquid in a pan over a high heat so that it bubbles strongly.

chill cooling food in a fridge.

combine mixing ingredients together evenly.

consistency how runny or thick a mixture is.

dice cutting an ingredient into small, equal cubes.

dissolve melting or liquifying a substance (often sugar in water).

dough the mixture of flour, water, sugar, and salt, before it is baked into bread.

drain removing excess liquid from food, often in a colander.

drizzle pouring slowly, in a trickle.

enzymes proteins made from amino acids that spark off chemical reactions in the body, such as breaking down lactose in milk.

fold mixing ingredients together gently, to keep the air in the mixture.

fry cooking food in oil.

grate shredding an ingredient into little pieces by rubbing it on a grater.

grease rubbing butter or oil onto a baking sheet, tin, or tray to stop food from sticking.

juice squeezing liquid out of a fruit or vegetable.

knead pressing and folding dough with your hands until it is smooth and stretchy. This distributes the yeast.

line placing baking parchment or foil in a tin or on a baking sheet, so that food won't stick to it.

lukewarm mildly warm.

mash crushing ingredients with a fork or masher.

melt heating a solid substance until it becomes a liquid.

mix combining ingredients together, either by hand or with equipment.

moist slightly wet.

muddle squashing and stirring ingredients to release their flavours.

peaks raised areas that look like the tops of mountains.

phytochemical a chemical compound made by plants.

pipe making a strip of icing as a decoration on a cake or cupcake.

portion an amount or helping of food.

preheat turning the oven on and heating it to the correct temperature before baking food in it.

process blending an ingredient or ingredients in a food processor.

proving the final rise of bread dough before baking.

pungent a strong, sharp taste or smell.

purée blending fruit or vegetables in a blender to make a thick pulp.

ripe when a fruit is soft and ready to be eaten.

rise dough gets bigger in size when left in a warm place.

roll out flattening out and shaping dough or pastry using a rolling pin.

rub in rubbing flour and butter together with your fingers to create a texture that looks like breadcrumbs.

season adding salt and freshly ground black pepper to a dish to add flavour.

set leaving food on the work surface, in the fridge, or in the freezer until it firms up and turns solid.

sift using a sieve to remove lumps from dry ingredients.

simmer cooking over a low heat, so that it is bubbling gently.

slice using a knife to cut food into strips.

sprinkle scattering a food lightly over another food.

stone removing the stone from fruit or vegetables.

transfer moving something from one place to another.

well a dip made in flour, in which to crack an egg or pour liquid into.

whisk evenly mixing ingredients together with a whisk.

yeast a type of fungus that, when added to flour, water, and salt, causes the mixture to rise.

zest the skin of a citrus fruit that has been grated with a grater or a zester.

Index

Acknowledgements

DORLING KINDERSLEY would like to thank the following people for their assistance in the preparation of this book: Anne Damerell for legal assistance, Laura Nickoll for proofreading, Helen Peters for compiling the index, Annabel Hartog for recipe testing, Carrie Love and Rachael Parfitt Hunt for photo shoot prop styling, Eleanor Bates, Rachael Hare, Becky Walsh, James King, Clare Lloyd, Abi Luscombe, Charlotte Milner, Seeta Parmar for assistance at photo shoots.

The publisher would also like to thank the following for their kind permission to reproduce their photographs:
(Key: a-above; b-below/bottom; c-centre; f-far; l-left; r-right; t-top)

6 Dreamstime.com: Ljupcho Jovkovski (clb) Cover images:
Front: 123RF.com: Jessmine ca; Dreamstime.com: Primopiano (Background); Back: Dreamstime.com: Primopiano (Background).